The Nature Kid's Guide to
OSTRICHES

DAVID ANDERSON

LP Media Inc. Publishing
Text copyright © 2026 by LP Media Inc.
All rights reserved.

For information address LP Media Inc. Publishing,
30012 Variolite St NW, Princeton MN 55371
www.lpmedia.org

Publication Data

Ostriches
The Nature Kid's Guide to Ostriches — First edition.

Summary: "Learn all about Ostriches, the Nature Kid Way"
— Provided by publisher.

ISBN: 979-8-89818-224-3

[1. Ostriches – Non-Fiction] I. Title.

Title: The Nature Kid's Guide to Ostriches

CONTENTS

Dusty Digs 4

African Homes 6

Super Sized 8

Bird Bodies 10

Sharp Sight 12

Kick Hard 14

Pick and Peck 16

Boom Calls 18

Hungry Hunters 20

Run Fast 22

Speed Stars 24

Day Life 26

Flock Fun 28

Dance Moves 30

Cute Chicks 32

Doting Dads 34

Tough Birds 36

Spot One 38

DUSTY DIGS

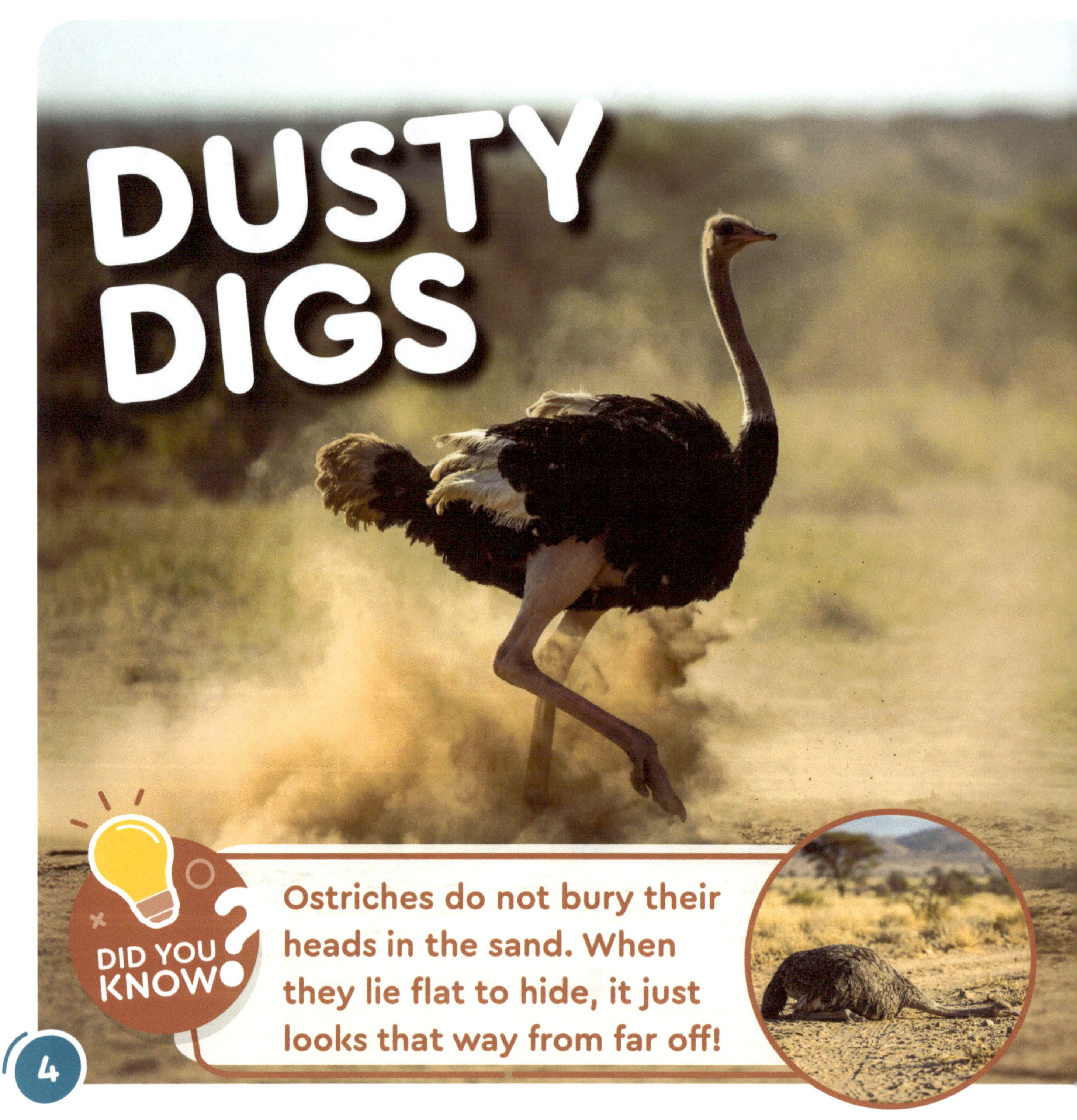

DID YOU KNOW?
Ostriches do not bury their heads in the sand. When they lie flat to hide, it just looks that way from far off!

Thump, thump! A tall ostrich stomps across the dusty plain.

Imagine a bird taller than your dad that can outrun a horse but cannot fly a single inch. That is an ostrich — the biggest bird on Earth and one of its most surprising animals.

Ostriches live across the hot open **plains** and sandy deserts of Africa, where the flat land stretches as far as you can see. They chose this landscape for a reason. With nothing to block the view, an ostrich can spot danger coming from miles away. No wings needed when you can see that far.

AFRICAN HOMES

Whoosh! A Somali ostrich dashes over the hot African grassland.

Ostriches live only in Africa. You will not find wild ones anywhere else! They roam the wilds of this big, sunny continent.

Some ostriches live in East Africa. Others live far to the south. The Somali ostrich is a special kind that lives near the east coast. Its neck and legs are blue-gray instead of pink!

Each group has its own area to call home. But all ostriches need open spaces with few trees and lots of room to roam.

SUPER SIZED

An ostrich is tall enough to peek over the roof of most cars. Imagine seeing those big eyes looking down at you!

Whump! A giant ostrich walks by, taller than any person around.

An ostrich can grow up to nine feet tall. That is almost as tall as a basketball hoop! It is the tallest bird on Earth.

A big male can weigh over 300 pounds. That is as heavy as two grown-ups! Females are a bit smaller, but still very big.

The North African ostrich is the largest kind of all. Even baby ostriches are big. When they hatch, they are already the size of an adult chicken! Everything about these birds is super sized!

BIRD BODIES
DID YOU KNOW?
Ostrich bones are solid and heavy, not hollow like most bird bones. That is one reason they cannot fly!

Flap, flap! An ostrich spreads its big, fluffy wings wide.

An ostrich has a tiny head on a long, bendy neck. Its round body is covered in soft feathers. Males are black and white. Females are light brown.

Each foot has only two toes. Most birds have three or four! One toe is extra big with a sharp claw. Their long legs have no feathers at all, just bare, scaly skin.

Ostriches use their wings in clever ways. They spread them wide to cool off in the heat. Wings also help them balance and steer when they run fast.

SHARP SIGHT

An ostrich can spot a moving lion from over two miles away!

Swish! An ostrich turns its head and spots a bug far away.

Ostriches have the biggest eyes of any land animal. Each eye is almost two inches wide. That is bigger than their own brain!

Those huge eyes are great for spotting danger. An ostrich can see things far off in the distance. This gives them plenty of time to run to safety.

Ostriches can also hear well. They listen for sounds from predators nearby. With good eyes and sharp ears, these birds stay alert every single day.

KICK HARD

One ostrich kick is strong enough to knock down a full-grown lion. Even hyenas know to keep their distance!

Wham! A mother ostrich kicks at a jackal with her strong leg.

Ostriches do not need to hide. They can fight back! Their legs are very powerful and built for kicking.

One kick from an ostrich can be deadly. The big toe on each foot has a four-inch claw. That sharp claw can slice through tough skin like a knife.

Even big animals stay away from an angry ostrich. A mother will kick hard to keep her babies safe. No predator wants to mess with those powerful legs!

PICK AND PECK

DID YOU KNOW?

An ostrich belly can hold over two pounds of stones. Those rocks work like a grinding machine inside!

Peck, peck! An ostrich snaps up seeds from the dry ground.

Ostriches eat many kinds of food. They munch on seeds, roots, and flowers. They also snack on bugs, lizards, and other small critters.

These birds grab food with their flat beaks. They swallow small stones, too! The stones sit in their belly and help grind up tough food since they have no teeth.

Ostriches spend a lot of time eating. They walk from spot to spot, pecking as they go. A hungry ostrich will try almost anything it can swallow!

BOOM CALLS

A booming ostrich call sounds a bit like a lion's roar. You can hear it from over a mile away!

Boom! A male ostrich lets out a deep, thundering call.

Male ostriches make a booming sound. It is so deep you can feel it in your chest! They puff up their necks to make this loud call.

Females make sounds too. They click and cluck to talk to each other. Hissing means stay away! Each sound has a different meaning.

Ostriches also use their bodies to show how they feel. They flap their wings and bob their heads. A raised neck means they feel strong and ready to fight.

HUNGRY HUNTERS

A cheetah is faster than an ostrich in a short sprint. But ostriches can run longer without getting tired!

Growl! A hungry cheetah creeps closer to the ostrich flock.

Lions are one of the biggest dangers to ostriches. Cheetahs and leopards hunt them too. Hyenas may also try to grab a young bird.

Eggs and chicks face the most danger. Jackals and vultures sneak in when parents look away. Even eagles may swoop down on a small chick.

But adult ostriches are hard to catch. They are big, fast, and can kick hard. Most hunters go after the young or the weak instead.

RUN FAST

An ostrich can zig and zag while running at full speed. Try catching something that fast and tricky!

Zoom! An ostrich spots danger and takes off in a flash!

When an ostrich senses danger, it runs! Running is the best way to stay safe. At full speed, an ostrich can run 45 miles per hour. That's three times faster than an Olympic sprinter.

An ostrich can keep running for 30 minutes without getting tired. Most predators have to stop and rest long before that.

Sometimes an ostrich lies flat on the ground to hide. Its body looks like a bump of dirt from far away. Staying still and low is another clever trick for staying safe.

SPEED STARS

Ostriches are the fastest animals on two legs in the whole world. No other bird even comes close!

Thud, thud! Giant ostrich feet pound the earth like drums.

Each step an ostrich takes covers a lot of ground. One **stride** can be up to 16 feet long. That is longer than a car!

Strong toes grip the dirt as they run. Their springy legs bounce them forward like pogo sticks. Wings spread out to help them balance and turn.

Ostriches travel for miles and miles each day. Their long legs carry them far with ease. Walking for an ostrich is like jogging for us!

DAY LIFE

Ostriches take dust baths to keep bugs off their skin. They roll and flap until they are covered in dirt!

26

Ruffle! An ostrich shakes dust off its feathers at sunrise.

Ostriches wake up when the sun rises. They spend the cool morning hours walking and looking for food. Pecking and searching keeps them busy.

When it gets very hot, they rest in the shade. They may sit down and take it easy for hours. The hottest part of the day is naptime!

As the sun goes down, they look for food again. Ostriches are active during the day and sleep at night. They tuck their heads close to the ground when they rest.

FLOCK FUN

Ostriches sometimes hang out with zebras and antelopes. More animals means more eyes watching for lions!

Cluck! A group of ostriches walks together across the plain.

Ostriches like to live in groups. A group of ostriches is called a **flock**. Most flocks have about 10 to 12 birds.

Each flock has one main male who is the leader. There is also a main female who helps keep the group in order. The other birds follow their lead.

Living in a group helps keep everyone safe. More eyes means more chances to spot danger. Ostriches in a flock take turns watching for trouble while others eat.

DANCE MOVES

A male ostrich turns his neck bright pink or red during mating season!

Swoosh! A male ostrich waves his big wings in a wild dance.

Male ostriches put on a big show to win a mate. They drop to their knees and swing their wings side to side. It looks like a silly, happy dance!

The male with the best moves gets picked. Females watch closely before they choose. A strong, healthy male is always the best dancer.

After mating, the main female lays her eggs in a big sandy nest. Other females may add their eggs too. One nest can hold a huge pile of eggs!

CUTE CHICKS

DID YOU KNOW?
An ostrich egg is so strong that a grown person can stand on it without cracking it!

Crack! A fuzzy baby ostrich pops its head out of a big egg.

Ostrich eggs are the biggest eggs in the world. One egg can weigh about three pounds. That is as heavy as 24 chicken eggs!

A baby ostrich is called a chick. It uses a special bump on its beak to break out of the shell. This can take hours of hard work! Chicks are covered in soft, spiky fluff.

Newborn chicks can walk and run soon after hatching. They follow their parents right away. Within days, they can keep up with the whole group.

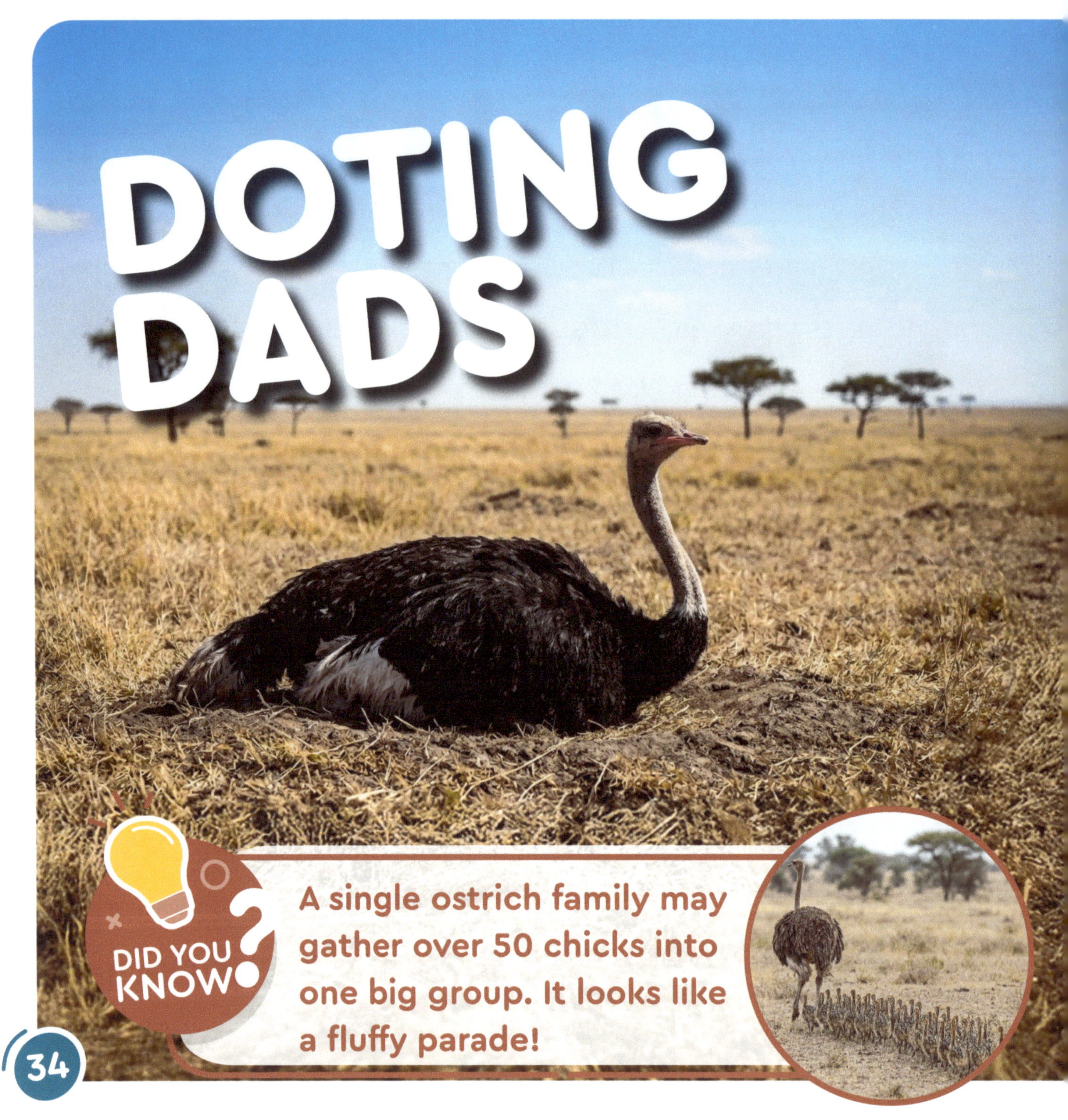

DOTING DADS

A single ostrich family may gather over 50 chicks into one big group. It looks like a fluffy parade!

Shh! A father ostrich sits quietly on a nest full of eggs.

Ostrich dads are super parents. The father sits on the eggs at night to keep them warm. His black feathers help him hide in the dark.

During the day, the mother takes a turn. Her lighter colors blend in with the sandy ground. Together, they keep the eggs safe for about 42 days.

Once the chicks hatch, the father leads them around. He shows them where to find food and water. He will fight any animal that gets too close to his babies.

TOUGH BIRDS

Ostriches can handle temperatures from over 100 degrees to below freezing. Now that is one tough bird!

Huff! An ostrich walks miles across the hot, dry desert.

Ostriches are built to survive tough times. They can go for days without a drink of water. They get what they need from the plants they eat.

Their bodies handle heat very well. They have a special way to cool their blood as they breathe. Even the hottest days do not slow them down.

Ostriches have lived on Earth for millions of years. They know how to find food in the driest places. These tough birds are true survivors.

SPOT ONE

Many zoos let you hand feed ostriches some seeds!

38

Click! A camera snaps a photo of a wild ostrich on safari.

A **safari** is the best way to see wild ostriches up close on the open African plains. But you do not have to travel to Africa to meet one!

Many zoos across the United States keep ostriches, and some even let you get close enough to hand feed them. When you visit, watch how they move, listen for their calls, and pay attention to how they use their eyes. Ask a zookeeper if there is a feeding time you can watch.

Seeing an ostrich in person is something you will never forget. There is simply no other bird like it on Earth.

GLOSSARY

safari

A trip to watch wild animals in their natural home, usually in Africa

flock

A group of birds that live and travel together

plain

A large, flat area of land with few trees

mate

A partner an animal chooses to have babies with

stride

One full step, measured from where one foot lands to where it lands again